Tony Turtle and Friends

Tony Turtle and Friends

Mary Bowyer

iUniverse, Inc.
New York Lincoln Shanghai

Tony Turtle and Friends

iUniverse, Inc.

For information address:
iUniverse, Inc.
2021 Pine Lake Road, Suite 100
Lincoln, NE 68512
www.iuniverse.com

ISBN: 0-595-32152-6

Printed in the United States of America

Contents

Tony Turtle

Tony Turtle was strolling through the garden
When he spied
A great big rock that had a hole
That he could hide inside.

Mom Turtle will never find me here, he thought.
I'll have my wishes
Of never having to eat my broccoli
Or help with dinner dishes.

So Tony Turtle crawled inside
But soon afterward he thought
Of how Mom Turtle stroked his shell
(He sure liked that a lot).

And how she patted his head
Before he went to bed, and kissed it
He used to think it kind of dumb
But now he sort of missed it.

He thought of Daddy Turtle
And the stories he would tell
Of brave, strong turtles long ago
Those stories sure were swell.

So Tony Turtle ran on home
To the sweet home that was his
Fast as a lightning thunderbolt
(For a small turtle, that is).

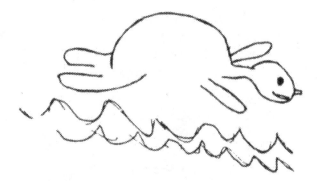

The Talking Towel

I rubbed my hands on the Talking Towel,
Was I surprised when he let out a howl
And told me that he had something to say
And could I kindly dry my hands another day.

He talked on and on about his life
About his kids and about his wife
To tell the truth he's talking yet
And my poor hands, they're still all wet.

Time Was

Time was when alligators flew
And ponies said "Cockadoodle-doo"
And dogs could sing
And mice had wings
There was a time when pigs went "mew."

But nowadays the cats "meow"
A mooing sound comes from a cow
The young birds sing
The geese have wings
I think the world is mixed up now.

Nelson Noodle

Nelson Noodle was so flat
As flat as he could be,
Upon a sea of soup he sat
And muttered gloomily.

"I'd love to run and jump and step
Instead of lying here,
If I could have a little pep
How full I'd be of cheer.

To jump and run and dance and sing
That is my fondest wish,
To roller skate, all full of zing
Not lie here in this dish.

Then Granny Noodle did appear
From noodleland on high,
She said, "You're perfect as you are
So, Nelson, don't ask why

You cannot run and skip and roll
Just like an ol' French poodle,
Just swim around in this fine bowl
And be proud to be a noodle."

Clickety-Plickety Rickety-Rum

Clickety-plickety rickety-rum
Bang on the cymbals, beat on the drum,
A dancing elf will surely come
Clickety-plickety rickety-rum.

Cuddly Bear

Cuddly Bear went to the store
To buy herself a bow,
To place atop her cuddly fur
So she would look just so.

But on arriving at the store
There were no bows in sight,
Just one small pair of roller skates
Which filled her with delight.

So 'stead of being Cuddly Bear
Whose looks compared to none,
She was Cuddly Bear on roller skates
(Which was a lot more fun!)

Little Piggy

Little Piggy ran and jumped,
Into the furniture he bumped.
He did a headstand on his snout,
He smiled and laughed and twirled about.

Little Tommy was delighted,
But Mommy was a little frighted.
"I don't know," she said to Dad,
"To clean up, what a time I've had."

But Little Tommy begged and pleaded,
So to his wishes Mom acceded.
The Piggy lived there ever after,
And the house was always filled with laughter.

OH MOMMY, DADDY,
CAN WE KEEP HIM?

What's a Moekling?

"What's a moekling?" asked the king.
"A moekling's part 'moek' and part 'ling.'
A moekling's small and loves to sing.
Or a moekling's big with golden wings.

A moekling has a ruddy snout,
And loves to laugh and roam about,
Among the trees, so you can see,
He's quite a lot like you and me."

"I think I see now," said the king.
"I'd love to have my own moekling."
"They're not for having, no siree,
For moeklings must always be free.

But if at night you close your eyes
And point your finger to the skies,
Your own moekling with furry head
Will cuddle with you in your bed."

Bobby Blanket

Bobby Blanket keeps me warm
He's my best friend in a thunderstorm.
I tell him all my joys and fears
He's always there to lend an ear.
And when I wiggle or I wuggle
He's always very glad to snuggle.

Little House

Little House sat on the hill
Feeling very sad and lonesome
For his owners had just moved away
And the weeds outside, they sure had grown some.

"Oh, woe is me," cried Little House,
"What is to become of me?
My stairs are creaking,
No one loves me
And the ants have eaten some of me.

My plaster's falling from the ceiling
My gates are getting worn and rusty.
It sure gives me an awful feeling
To say nothing of my smell, so musty."

His chimney shook with unshed tears
Then he just broke right down and cried,
When suddenly a Lovely Lady
Singing softly stepped inside.

"I'll fix you up, you precious house,"
She very sweetly, softly said.
Oh! Little House was so excited
That night he couldn't stay in bed.

She cleaned and mopped
And fixed and pruned
And swept the floors with sweeps so sweeply.
Now Little House is very gay
For Lovely Lady loves him deeply.

Sammy Seal

Sammy Seal lay basking in the sun
His day of chasing fish and such was done.
He heard a gentle splash of water
Spied a fish and nearly caught her.
When she spoke up (from safely on the run).

"Oh, Sammy Seal, why do you chase me?
To eat me up is just to waste me.
Let's bring this killing to an end
And let me be your little friend."

Sammy pondered the small fish's wish
(He'd never before been friends with a fish).
But she was so sweet, with a big smile so grand
He put out his fin to shake her sweet hand.

Now they swim fin in hand over Life's lovely seas
And Sam and the fish are both very pleased.
For they've learned that the problems of fishship and menship
Can be solved by one thing and one thing only: Friendship.

The Little Pig

The little pig
Did dance a jig
Quite upside down
In his pigsty.
He danced with Mortimer, the cat
With Dick, the horse
And Bert, the fly.
He danced till he could dance no more
Then said, "Oh, what a pig am I."

I Met Mr. Bear

I met Mr. Bear,
He was hungry and mean.
He said, "I would eat you,
But you're really too lean.
Here's a chocolate éclair,
Make you fit for a bear."
But I said, "N-N-No, I really must go.
I really would try it
But I'm on a strict diet,
I get th-thinner each day."
And I scooted away.

Pistachio Pillow

Pistachio Pillow sat on the bed
Patiently waiting for little Tim's head.
He let out a sigh
When he heard Timmy cry
"One more story, Mom!"
(That's the tenth one she read!)
An impatient and lonesome Pistachio said.

The Sweet Little Rowboat

The sweet little rowboat
Was lost at sea.
"Oh, my," she cried
"What will happen to me?"
She got ate by a whale
And got stuck in his tale,
But got blown out his mouth
By the next gusty gale.
She rowed and she rowed,
She at last reached the shore.
"It's lagoons from now on,"
She said—forevermore.

Shoop, Shoop, Noodle Soup

Shoop, shoop
Noodle soup,
Drink it when you start to droop.
Scoop the noodles with a scoop,
Shoop, shoop,
Noodle soup.

It's good for slurping right out loud
To quite impress a great big crowd.
It's good for sprinkling at your dad
(Although he might get slightly mad.)
Shoop, shoop
Noodle soup.
Drink it when you start to droop.

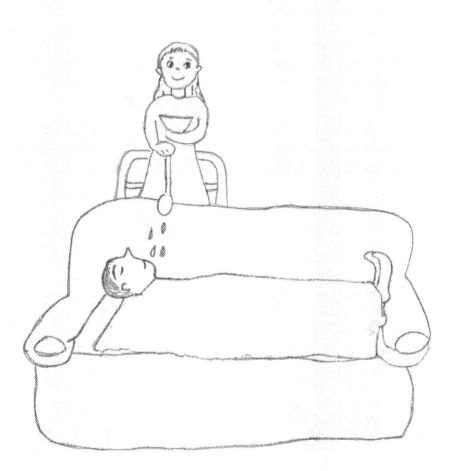

Sing, Sing, Little Bird

Sing, sing, little bird.
Sing, sing little bird.
Your song is so special,
It needs to be heard.
Your song is so lovely,
A song without words.
Sing, sing, little bird.
Sing, sing, little bird.

Chatter-to-Ya

Chatter-to-ya, scatter-to-ya,
Tell me, what's it matter to ya?
That I caught the biggest bear,
That ever lumbered anywhere?
That I caught the biggest fish
To ever sit on any dish?
That I eat my meals on wheels
And never walk but on my heels?
Chatter-to-ya, scatter-to-ya,
Tell me, what's it matter to ya?

Kotch Kitty

Kotch Kitty sat on a pile of papers
Trying to think up some brand new capers.
It came to him like the light of dawn
"I'll eat the papers I'm sitting upon."

"I'll start with the one that is nearest my head,"
And as he was chewing, he silently read.
Now the papers are gone—only trace that you'll find
Is stored up inside Kotch's mischievous mind.

Long Fellow

I saw a fellow
Long and thin
Who had the very widest grin.
And when he smiled from side to side
As long as he was, his grin was as wide!

Twinky T'wosy

Twinky T'wosy
Has a nosey
Longer than a row of darts.
And when she runs around the block
Her nose gets home before *she* starts.

Terrific

I feel terrific
Quite splentific
Almost feel that I could fly.
I feel so yummy
Filled my tummy
With a cherry pie on rye.

I feel so, so good
Nothing's no good
Feel like diving in a pool.
My teacher told us,
Smiled and told us,
That tomorrow there's no school.

Silly Willy

Silly Willy went to Philly.
Maybe he is still-y there.
For Philly has the neatest music
And the greatest county fair.

Silly Willy rode a red horse
There at Philly's county fair,
And Silly Willy won't step down
From Philly's filly, will he?

Mary Bowyer

Mommy Mousie

Mommy Mousie had a tail,
Longer than a city mile.
All her little mousie babes,
Jumped rope with it, it made her smile.

Tic-y, Tac-y, Toe-y

Tic-y, tac-y, toe-y,
I have a friend named Joey,
And everywhere we go-y,
Through wind or rain or snow-y,
If it's sunny or it's blow-y,
Together's how we go-y,
Just me and my friend, Joey,
Tic-y, tac-y, toe-y.

Johnny Jello

Johnny Jello couldn't jiggle
Not even the slightest wiggle
He sat in his bowl, quite an unhappy fellow
For if Jell-O can't jiggle, it hardly is Jell-O.

Then one day, the Jiggling Godmother walked past
Saw Johnny and set him to jiggling real fast
Now Johnny not only wiggles and jiggles
He's so very happy, that he even giggles.

Timoctopus Octopus

Timoctopus Octopus
Had eight long arms,
He sang to the fishes
With all of his charms.
The fish loved his song
And they shouted—More! More!
So he bowed quite politely
And did an encore.

Minula Mousie

Minula Mousie sat and wondered,
Why it rained and poured and thundered.
She sat for hours pondering
The flash and noise that rainstorms bring.
"It must be giant mice above
A 'fighting with their boxing gloves
That makes the thunder groan and growl
And clap and shriek and shout and howl.
And when one giant mousie wins,
Exactly then—the rain begins.
The losing mousie just sits and cries
And pours down teardrops from the skies,
Till once again Dame Sun does rise
To dry his red and swollen eyes.

China Cup and Chandelier

China Cup and Chandelier
Engaged in conversation.
Said Chandelier to China Cup,
"I need a sweet libation."

Said China Cup to Chandelier
"Come hither, drink my brew.
And if you do not mind too much
I'll ask a favor of you.

I'm sitting in the kitchen, dark
Without a bit of light.
Please shine on me, a tiny spark
To brighten up my night."

"Most certainly," said Chandelier,
"You are my friend and so,
I'll shine for you the brightest light
To set your heart aglow."

He shone his light, and sipped his brew
(Which filled him with delight)
And watched as China fell asleep
Then, soft, turned out the light.

Ben Balloon

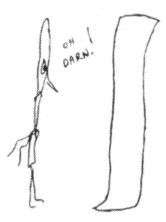

Ben Balloon was very sad, for he was flat as could be.
Not nice and round and full of air like proper balloons should be.
Every day he glanced in the mirror to see if he'd got fat
And every day he sadly saw that he was still as flat.

Then one bright day Anne Airful came and blew him up so round,
That now he floats ten thousand million feet above the ground.
He hobnobs with the clouds and stars, they tell him lovely tales,
And if you look 'way, 'way up high, you'll see him as he sails.

There Was a Little Butterfly

There was a little butterfly
Who wanted so to reach the sky.
All day she'd flap her wings and try,
But only climbed a few feet high.
Then suddenly there came a word
Of wisdom from a little bird.
He said, "My friend, don't just aspire
To fly higher and yet higher,
But make the most of each inch flown.
Your flight is not only your own,
But visit with each tree and flower
And bring each one a happy hour.
Then the butterfly flew here and there
Spreading kind words everywhere,
Leaving seeds of caring deeds
With trees, with flowers, even weeds.
She cared no more to reach the skies
The butterfly had grown so wise.
She'd gained real joy, she'd gained real bliss
By sharing love and happiness.

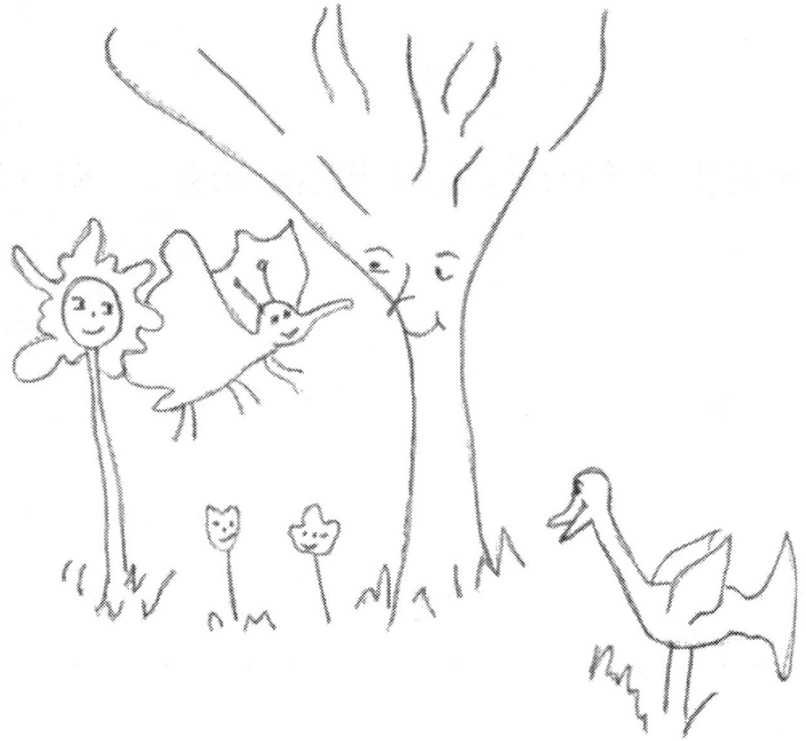

0-595-32152-6

Printed in the USA
CPSIA information can be obtained
at www.ICGtesting.com
JSHW022240030324
58157JS00023B/79

9 780595 321520